DISCARDED BY
EPL

EUROPEAN PIPES

by

Roger Fresco-Corbu

Series Editor: Noël Riley

LUTTERWORTH PRESS
Guildford, Surrey

First published 1982

Cover illustration shows porcelain bowl with
metal lid, European mid-19th century, and English
clay late 19th century. Photo: Cedric Bush

All black and white photographs taken by
Nicholas Mackenzie

The Publishers apologize to the National Magazine Co. Ltd. for
unintentionally using their trade mark 'Antique Collector' in the
series title of this book which has no connection with their
'Antique Collector' magazine.

ISBN 0 7188–2535–7

Copyright © Roger Fresco-Corbu 1982
Illustrations © Lutterworth Press 1982

No part of this book may be reproduced in
any form, by print, photoprint, microfilm
or any other means without written permission
from the publisher.

Printed in Great Britain by
Mackays of Chatham Ltd

Contents

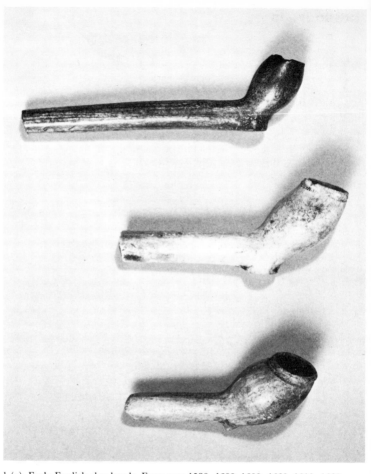

1 (a) Early English clay bowls. From top: 1580–1600, 1600–1620, 1610–1630. All the stems are broken.

Introduction

TOBACCO was unknown in the Old World until the discovery of America, where the various species of the plant seemed to thrive in several regions, both in North and South America.

The story begins on a day in November 1492 when Rodrigo de Jerez and Luis de Torres, two members of the Columbus expedition, were put ashore to explore an island and there saw natives smoking what appeared to be bundles of dry leaves. The leaves we now know to have been tobacco and the island in question was Cuba. The 450th anniversary of the discovery of America was commemorated belatedly by Cuba in 1944 with the issue of a set of stamps dated 1492–1942. The large 10 centavos violet portrays two astonished Spaniards looking at the recumbent figure of a huge native leaning his head and shoulders against a tree and smoking a big cigar. The stamp is captioned in Spanish 'Jerez and Torres discover tobacco'.

It took many more expeditions and about half a century for the tobacco leaf and seed to reach Europe via Portugal and Spain. In the

1 (*b*) English clay 1680–1700. Length 5½ in., depth of bowl 1⅜ in.

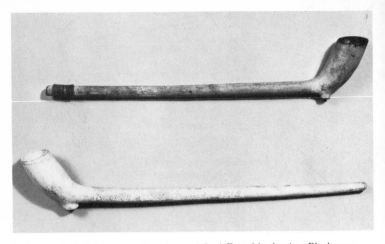

2. Two typical 18th century clay pipes. (*above*) Found in the river Blackwater at Bradwell-on-Sea, Essex. Length 8½ in. Depth of bowl 1¾ in. 1730–1750. (*below*) Facsimile of a pipe dated 1715; made in 1915 and inscribed on reverse 'The Bi-centenary Pipe'.

beginning its use was purely medicinal and many curative properties were wrongly attributed to it. By the closing decades of the 16th century, however, 'drinking tobacco', as smoking was then called, had become the indulgence it is today.

The American Indian custom of smoking tobacco in pipes quickly reached Europe and the first pipes were essentially functional and closely resembled one of the types commonly found in America. Before long ornamentation began to be applied and this increased over the centuries, reaching a peak during the 19th century.

Whether a pipe is a cheaply moulded clay or an artistically carved meerschaum, its chief interest from the collector's point of view lies in the social or historical background responsible for its creation rather than in its monetary value.

In order to give the reader a general idea of

the collecting possibilities in this vast field within the compass of a comparatively small book, it has been necessary to omit a number of interesting types of pipes. The choice of what to leave out has been the most difficult part of an otherwise very enjoyable task. Wherever possible I have tried to make amends by illustrating and captioning some items not mentioned in the text. Apologies are offered to those who do not find a favourite specimen described or illustrated.

1.   The Clay Pipe in England

THE identity of the man who first brought tobacco to England has been a subject of debate among historians over the centuries. The great Elizabethan sea captains Drake, Hawkins and Raleigh have all had their advocates and so has Ralph Lane, the first governor of Virginia.

William Harrison, writing of the year 1573 in his *Great Chronologie* (1588) says that:

'In these days the taking in of the smoke of the Indian herbe called *Tabaco* by an instrument formed like a little ladell, where-

3. Large clay pipe intended for display rather than for smoking. Designed by C. Crop of London and registered on March 17, 1862, in time for the International Exhibition in May. It depicts the exhibition building and is impressed with the registration of design mark, maker's name and 'Exhibition 1862'.
(*below*) The same pipe seen from underneath.

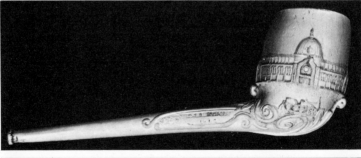

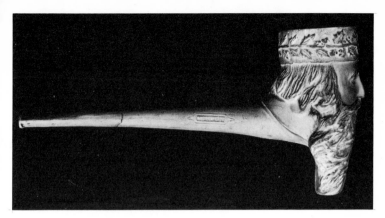

4. Large clay pipe of Father Christmas. His hat is decorated with holly leaves and berries. These are slightly coloured green and red (an unusual feature in English clay pipes). Made by C. Crop of London 1870–1880. Length about 8¼ in. Depth of head 4 in.

by it passeth from the mouth into the head and stomach, is gretlie taken-up and used in England against Rheums and some other diseases engendered in the lungs and inward parts, and not without effect.'

It would thus appear that tobacco was being used in England as early as 1573; the popularly held belief attributing its introduction to Raleigh cannot therefore be valid since Sir Walter's expeditions to the New World did not start until 1584. The strongest claimant seems to be Sir John Hawkins and his crew, on the return from his second voyage in 1565. This assertion cannot be conclusively proved either, although it is based on a few near contemporary sources. There is little doubt however that it was Sir Walter Raleigh, explorer, diplomat and royal favourite who, by his enthusiasm for the weed, made pipe smoking not only popular but also socially acceptable.

There are no reliable records relating to the

5. (*above*) General Kitchener. Design registered by C. Crop in 1898 and intended to commemorate Kitchener's victory at the Battle of Omdurman.

6. (*below*) Queen Mary. Commemorating the Coronation in 1911.

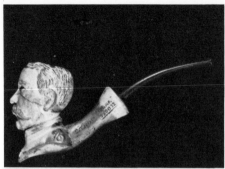

very first clay-pipe makers in England; it would appear that manufacture started some time during the late 1560s or early 1570s. There is ample evidence that manufacture increased steadily as the century advanced. Many more records are available from the early years of the 17th century onwards and in 1619 the tobacco-pipe makers of London became an incorporated body and were granted arms.

Through the efforts of many distinguished archaeologists working during the 19th and 20th centuries, and culminating in recent years with the researches of Adrian Oswald, a pipe typology has been evolved. Oswald, in addition to his own studies, has collated regional monographs by other keen students of the subject in his *magnum opus* entitled *Clay Pipes for the Archaeologist* (*see* p. 62).

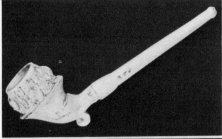

7. (*above*) Cornucopia pipe. Early 20th century.

8. (*below*) Football pipe. Late 19th or early 20th century.

The features on which the typology is based are a combination of shape and size of bowl, slope of bowl in relation to stem, form of base (spur, platform and so on), thickness of stem, size and position of stem-bore in relation to the centre, ornament, and makers' marks when available. This enables the experienced collector to date old clay pipes within a comparatively small bracket of twenty or thirty years.

As a general rule the bowls of the earliest pipes were very small and had a pronounced forward slope (fig. 1). The size increased over the years and the slope decreased until, at some time in the 18th century, the top of the bowl became almost parallel with the stem. During the 19th century a slight slope appears again but pipes of this period have much more slender stems than those of the previous centuries and should therefore not be

9. (*above*) Shakespeare 1930.

10. (*below*) John Bull, late 19th or early 20th century.

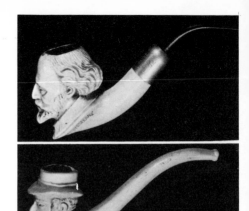

confused with them (fig. 2).

The base of the bowl consisted at first of a flat oval or circular heel (pear-shaped on the pipes made at Broseley in Shropshire). This formed a continuation of the stem until about 1600–1610 when it started to be stepped down. The flat base gradually gave way to a spur and this too had mostly disappeared by the mid-19th century, when the present-day style began to predominate.

Until the early years of the 18th century most bowls had an incised line, a double line or a milled line round the top and this was, usually, the only form of decoration. From about the middle of the century raised ornament which included a spike of wheat, reeding or dots began to appear and went on increasing in variety throughout the next century. During the second half of the 19th century we find depicted activities ranging from politics to sport, ballooning, railways, regimental insignia and emblems of towns, societies and so on (figs. 5–14).

Marks, mostly in the form of makers' initials on the flat base, on either side of the spur or on the back or side of the bowl, and often the full name on the stem, have appeared on pipes from the earliest days. They were few at first but increased in numbers over the centuries, becoming quite common during the 19th century.

A very prolific firm was that of Charles Crop which was manufacturing in London between 1856 and 1924 (figs. 3–5). Many of their designs were registered and were therefore impressed with the diamond-shaped registration mark or number from which the date of the original mould can be determined. The name C. Crop, with or without 'London', was usually impressed on their pipes.

This firm produced models of many contemporary personalities at home and abroad, from royalty to political figures and military

11. (*above*) Design registered in 1908 by Parnell of Plaistow. Length – 5½ in. Height 3½ in.

12. (*centre*) Tower Bridge in relief. Made for the Tower Bridge Hotel, early this century.

13. (*below*) Badge of the Inniskilling regiment. Produced by several makers from the last quarter of the 19th century onwards.

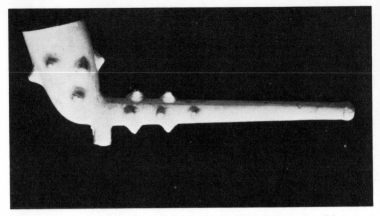

14. A popular design during the last quarter of the 19th century and well into this century.

heroes. The various campaigns in South Africa, from the Zulu Wars of the 1870s to the Boer War of 1899–1902, were portrayed by this factory. Among popular busts used at the time were those of Baden-Powell, French and Kitchener. The Dreyfus affair in France created a wave of sympathy in Britain for that unfortunate officer, wrongly accused of spying, and Crop produced a Captain Dreyfus pipe in 1894, the year of his trial.

Writing about pipes with long stems, Fairholt (*see* p. 62) says: 'Such long pipes were reverently termed "aldermen" in the last age, and irreverently "yards of clay" in this one'. Not long after this was written 'churchwarden' became the accepted designation for these pipes.

More than 6,000 makers who worked throughout the British Isles at some time or other are listed by Oswald. Today the clay pipe has only a very small number of devotees and their wants are supplied by the mere handful of workers still involved in this ancient craft.

2. Other English Pipes

Pottery. The coiled snake-like Staffordshire pipes (figs. 15 and 19) are typically English but a lot of research is still required in order to establish exactly who made them and where. We know roughly when they were made because a few were inscribed with the owner's name or initials and a date within the first quarter of the 19th century. Some had only two or three coils while other pipes consisted of a mass of spaghetti-like convolutions. Their colourful glazed decoration is reminiscent of other contemporary Staffordshire productions. It must be remembered that Staffordshire is a generic rather than specific term and applies to items originally made in the Potteries but later manufactured in several

15. (*left*) Staffordshire pottery pipe. Early 19th century.
16. (*right*) English salt-glazed stoneware pottery pipe. Length 4½ in.

17. Salt-glazed stoneware representation of Joseph Grimaldi, the famous clown, from Brampton, Derbyshire. Early 19th century.

other parts of the British Isles.

The snake pipes, so called because of their reptilian appearance, were more an amusing whimsy than a serious smoking utensil. It would be very difficult to draw the smoke through the long and involved tubing and even if this were possible the pipe could never be cleaned after use. In the simplest examples the snake's tail formed the mouthpiece while the creature's wide open mouth held the bowl, often decorated with human or animal faces.

The anonymous potters who made snake pipes were also probably responsible for another group of equally colourful pipes in the form of grotesque people or monkeys in human costume. The figures held in their mouths a pipe with a disproportionately large bowl, capable of taking enough tobacco for a good smoke, while the mouthpiece projected unnaturally from their backs (fig. 16).

Grotesque upright pipes were also made in

18. Wedgwood jasper ware pipe bowl. Impressed 'Wedgwood AA?'. The year letter is not clear. Possibly O or C. C. 1860s.

19. English salt-glazed stoneware pottery snake pipe. First half of the
19th century. Length 10 in.

brown salt-glazed stoneware pottery, mostly
at Brampton in Derbyshire, but also at a
number of other centres such as Fulham,
Lambeth, Nottingham and Portobello near
Edinburgh (fig. 17).

Some of these works also made the portable
stoneware pipes which were in vogue between
about the 1840s and the 1860s and portrayed
caricatures of humans, monkeys and other
creatures (fig. 20). A reference to one of the
latter is found in a small book *The Decked-
Welled Fishing Boat* by Henry Dempster, published in 1868. A pipe shaped like a sword-fish
is mentioned:

'The body of the fish is a vacuum; the sword
is represented by the pipe-shank, and the
tail of the fish turned upwards forms the
bowl of the pipe. . . . It was manufactured at
Portobello by a potter there but none have
been made for some years past.'

Wedgwood pipe bowls, in the firm's well-
known jasper, basalt and red wares, were
made on a few occasions during the 19th
century. They usually consisted of the bowl for
tobacco and a small reservoir for drainage
screwed on at the base (fig. 18).

20. (*left*) English decorative clear glass pipe. Length 10 in. First half of the 19th century.

21. (*centre*) Large pottery bowl (4¾ in.) representing the Victorian magazine character Alley Sloper. Created in the 1870s he remained popular until the early years of this century.

22. (*right*) Green glass pipe, 9½ in., first half of the 19th century.

Glass. From the glass works of Stourbridge, Bristol and Nailsea, came pipes in clear, opaque, red, green, blue or striped glass, displaying the skills of the glass-blower's art but not intended for smoking since the heat would crack them. Many were very large and showy and destined to adorn some late Georgian or early Victorian tobacconist's window (figs. 20, 22).

3.   French Clay Pipes of the 19th Century

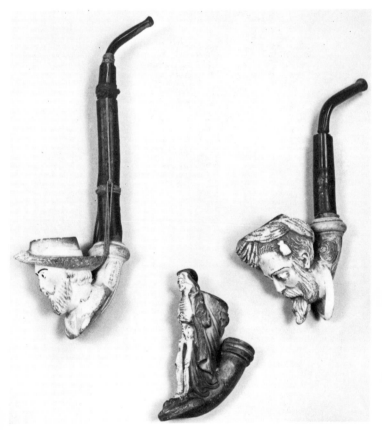

23. (*left*) French clay pipe bowl from the Gambier factory, representing Rubens.
Cherry-wood tube with horn mouthpiece.

24. (*right*) A Gambier head of an Algerian.

25. (*centre*) Mid-19th century *memento mori* clay from the Fiolet factory at
St Omer in France. Height 3¾ in.

26. Head of a drunkard described in the Gambier catalogue of 1894 as *Nez-Rouge* ('Red Nose').

ALL the clay pipes made in France until the early 19th century followed the conventional designs of the other West European countries, but then French makers started to produce the representational pipes known today as 'French clays'.

It is not clear which of the firms manufacturing at that time was responsible for this new development, but it would be fairly safe to credit either Gambier, the greatest of them all, established at Givet in the Ardennes by 1780, or Fiolet of St Omer, founded in 1765.

The bowls were moulded to represent both famous and infamous contemporary or historical characters, in France or abroad. There were rulers, politicians, writers, actors and military men, including among great generals men of humbler rank. One such was Sergeant Jules Bobillot, who died heroically in the Tonkin campaign of 1885. Mythological and legendary characters were also portrayed. All kinds of animals, birds, flowers and vegetables, skulls and skeletons, were depicted on these pipes. The range is enormous. Artistic merit apart, their main charm lies in

27. (*left*) Country-cottage scene in clay by Duméril, Leurs of St Omer, a comparatively short-lived firm (1845–1885).

28. (*right*) Gambier head of Pomona, mythical deity of fruit and gardens.

29. The Duke of Wellington. After the Duke's anti-smoking order to the Army in 1845 this pipe, lampooning the great soldier, was ordered by a Mr Benda, city tobacconist and pipe importer. It was made in 1846 by the firm of Duméril, Leurs of St Omer. Height of bowl 3 in.

the way in which they illustrate the political and social history of their day (figs. 23–40).

Spire Blondel, a French authority on the subject, writing in 1891 said that the earliest of these pipes could be seen in the Carnavalet Museum in Paris. One of them, representing Dr Deneux, surgeon to the Duchesse de Berry, could be dated to 1817. Blondel felt that there should be some earlier pipes of this type in existence, but had been unable to trace any in either private or public collections. He also stated that bowls representing notorious characters of the French Revolution of 1789 were not contemporary, but were mostly made during the uprising of 1848 and were an indication of the popular revolutionary feeling of the period.

Today, many years after these statements

30. Nicolas I of Montenegro fashioned in a red clay by Bonnaud of Marseilles in c. 1890.

21

31. A model by Gisclon of Lille made in *c.*1870. Overall length 8½ in.

32. Frédéric Soulié, the French novelist, first issued by Gambier in about 1845 and based on a caricature by Dantan. It is a play on words, *soulier* being French for shoe. The shoe is 3½ in. long.

were made, that first date of 1817 still stands, but research continues optimistically in the hope of discovering some ancient long-lost letter or document that may push the date back by a year or two.

Fairholt, in his 1859 book writes with great enthusiasm about French clay pipes. Speaking about the artists employed by the firm of Gambier, he says:

'They have produced the best and largest works; some of them are admirably modelled, and deserve preservation as art manufactures. A head of Silenus is particularly good. Fiolet of St Omer is his only legitimate rival and he has executed a vast variety of designs, many exceedingly good. Dumeril, who also has his works at St Omer, has produced some characteristic things. . . . Enamel glazes of various colours are sparingly introduced in most of these pipes, a general tinge of brown pervades the clay from the tobacco oil in smoking, but the part coated with the colours is preserved from its effects. A white enamel is constantly used for the eyes of these figures.'

Louis Fiolet, the founder's grandson, took over the firm on his father's death in 1834 and became the greatest of them all at St Omer. It was his wife who was responsible for introducing the colouring in enamels which became such a feature of many French clays during the 19th and early 20th centuries. Louis Fiolet stayed in charge until his death in 1892, when he was succeeded by his son-in-law Georges Audebert.

Some of the pipes had the stem and bowl moulded in one piece (fig. 27), but mostly they consisted of pipe-heads smoked by means of a cherry-wood stem terminating in a horn mouthpiece (figs. 23, 24 and 31). For small bowls there were short stems of horn or turned wood (fig. 29).

33. The French sculptor François Rude, a mid-19th century model by Fiolet of St Omer.

34. The actor Frédéric Lemaître in his theatrical interpretation of Robert Macaire, a boastful but rather amusing fictional rogue. Made by the firm of Blanc-Garin & Guyot of Givet in the Ardennes c.1835.

Large numbers of these clays were marked and can, therefore, be attributed to a maker. The usual Gambier mark was 'Gambier à Paris' and/or the letters JG impressed within a circle. One also finds Gambier in cursive writing incised on the shank of the bowl. In addition to the firm's name there is often a mould number, a practice adopted by most French manufacturers. It must be noted here that this firm made pipes only at Givet in the Ardennes, whereas the centre for their large distributing and co-ordinating organization was in Paris. They also had a London agency between 1860 and 1896.

Pipes by Fiolet were marked with one or both of the following in raised or impressed letters: 'L. Fiolet, St. Omer' or 'LF' in a circle. Duméril functioned from 1845 to 1895 and used a few variants of Duméril Leurs, St Omer, while Blanc-Garin & Guyot of Givet usually marked in a raised oval during their comparatively short existence between 1830 and 1860. Collectors may also find the mid-19th century mark of the Rennes manufac-

35. Bust of Bayard, the famous French soldier and hero, killed in battle in 1524. Moulded on the underside of the base is a panoply of arms. Issued by Gambier in the second quarter of the 19th century. Height 3¾ in.

36. Unmarked French clay pipe bowl representing an unidentified churchman.

turers Crétal-Gaillard, Gisclon (*c.* 1820–1880) of Lille, Bonnaud of Marseilles and, with luck, others. The last-mentioned firm functioned well into this century and was noted for models in red and black clays, often decorated with gilding (fig. 40).

Dating presents rather a problem. A mould once produced could be used for many years and the most thorough research can only establish the year of its creation. One would then have to decide the period during which the character depicted remained popular enough to make continued manufacture commercially viable. If dating bowls representing contemporary personalities is difficult, the problem is greatly increased with portrayals of other subjects unless they come from relatively short-lived firms such as Duméril or Blanc-Garin. Not all firms, however, are so

37. A Gambier head of Silenus. First produced in the second quarter of the 19th century.

25

38. (*left*) A Gambier probably designed for the American market and representing the American politician Bryan, defeated by Taft in the 1908 presidential election. The pipe was made a few years earlier.

39. (*right*) Early 20th century clay by Gambier, decorated with white and coloured enamel paint.

40. A dark brown clay was used by Bonnaud of Marseilles to fashion this biblical patriarch. Slight touches of gilding. Late 19th century.

well documented and the principal establishments spanned much more than a century.

The most common of all French clays represents the bearded and turbanned biblical patriarch Jacob and is inscribed 'JACOB' on the bowl. It was created by Gambier about the 1840s, and achieved such instant and sustained popularity that its manufacture by that firm, and numerous imitators, continued in several sizes until the 1920s.

With the increasing popularity of the more portable briar, the demand for clays began to wane in the early years of this century and the decline was accelerated by the First World War. The end came in the 1920s when the two greats, Fiolet and Gambier, closed down within five years of each other in 1921 and 1926 respectively.

4. The Porcelain Pipes of Germany and Neighbouring Countries

41. German pipe with matching floral decoration on porcelain bowl and reservoir. Stem – a combination of wood and horn. Overall length, 10 in., second half of the 19th century.

T HE smoking habit was introduced into Germany by the English troops under the command of Sir Horace Vere, who were sent in 1620 to the assistance of Frederick V, King of Bohemia, by his father-in-law James I of England. Once introduced, pipe-smoking spread to such an extent that Hans Jakob von Grimmelhausen – a chronicler of the Thirty Years War – was able to say that by the end of the war, in 1648, nine workmen out of ten smoked and that there was not a peasant's home in Germany without a tobacco pipe. The pipes smoked in Germany until the middle of the 18th century were mostly clays imported from Holland and England or made in Germany in the then fashionable Dutch styles.

In about the 1750s there appeared a new type of purely German manufacture – the porcelain pipe. This spread throughout the German-speaking countries and also to Holland, Scandinavia and, to a much lesser extent, France. The exact date of the invention, as with many other artefacts, is difficult to establish. It is likely that the first porcelain bowls were made at the Nymphenburg factory in Bavaria. A number of splendid specimens are recorded as the work of Franz Anton Bustelli, the artist employed there from 1756 to 1764.

In an old auction-sale catalogue five Bustelli pipes are listed and the following description of one item is typical of their workmanship:

'Modelled as a man's mask and with rococo scrolls and wave ornament in high relief, decorated in natural colours, pink and gold, mounted with metal-gilt lip, pierced cover and border chased with scrolls and foliage.'

42. (*left*) Porcelain pipe bowl with metal lid, mid-19th century portrait of a lady. Length 5¼ in.

43. (*right*) Porcelain bowl decorated with the portrait of a lady. According to an inscription on the back it was presented by 'A. Behrnauer to his I. Wainwright Heidelberg 1840'.

The Meissen porcelain factory records refer to pipe-heads for the first time in 1765 but by the end of the decade they were being made in some numbers both at Meissen and Nymphenburg. Before long they were also being fabricated at Fulda and Berlin and by the end of the century their manufacture had spread to the other German-speaking countries.

The earliest of these pipes were moulded in relief but as time went on the main ornament became a painting on the plain bowl of the pipe; a few, however, continued to be made in the old style. With the invention of underglaze transfer-printing in colours, about the middle of the 19th century, this new and faster method of decoration began to replace painting in all but the best factories.

Porcelain, unlike other pipe materials, is

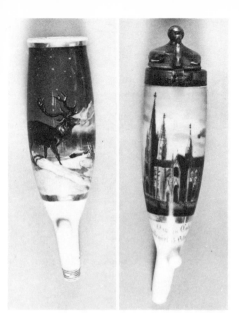

44. (*left*) Winter scene with stag in foreground, possibly after a painting. German porcelain *c.*1840s.

45. (*right*) Lidded porcelain bowl depicting Cologne Cathedral and commemorating its completion on October 15, 1880. Length 6 in.

non-absorbent and this caused the oils from the tobacco to drain to the bottom of the bowl, making it foul very quickly. Various experiments in design were tried in order to obviate this inconvenience. In one type the bowls were enlarged at the bottom forming a reservoir below the level of the stem fitting.

The model which to this day typifies the Germanic pipe was arrived at in about the 1760s or 1770s and was based on experiments carried out by a Dr Vicario of Lauffenburg in relation to wooden pipes. These tests would appear to have taken place in the late 17th or early 18th century. Vicario's work is mentioned in a German book entitled *Toback* compiled by one 'J.G.H.' and published at Chemnitz in 1719. The design consisted of a separate Y-shaped reservoir made usually of porcelain but also occasionally of horn, bone,

wood or metal. The bowl fitted into one leg of the Y by means of its short stalk-like extension, and the stem or tube in the other. The great advantage of this system was the ease with which the reservoir could be cleaned (fig. 41).

The stems, referred to as tubes (*Rohr*) in German, were made of wood, horn, bone, antler, ivory and metals or a combination of these materials, and ranged in length from a few inches to a few feet. Cherry was the favourite among woods, particularly for plain stems. Some of the more ornate long stems were made of several separate pieces, of one or more materials threaded at their ends so that they could be taken apart for cleaning. The mouthpiece, usually of horn, was often attached to the top of the stem by a piece of flexible tubing consisting of a wire spiral

46. (*above*) Porcelain bowl and plain reservoir of a German student pipe. The length of the stem would range up to 3 ft. Decorated with a panoply of crossed pipes, swords and so on, with the opening line of *Gaudeamus Igitur* the universal student song. Mid-19th century. Overall length 8 in.
47. (*left*) Transfer-printed scene of the Battle of Waterloo. The battle took place in 1815 but the bowl would be of a much later date, nearer the end of the century.
48. (*right*) General von Moltke (1800–1891). Bowl made *c.*1870.

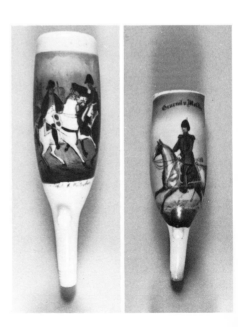

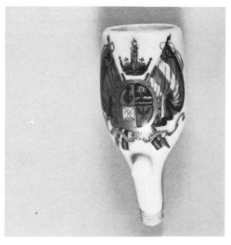

49. Armorial design presented, according to an inscription on the back, to E. Buch in 1869 and signed by fourteen participants in the presentation.

50. (*below*) German student driving wooden boot-trees into his jack-boots. Mid-19th century.

covered by several layers of coarsely woven material with an outside cover of very fine webbing.

Bowls were frequently fitted with metal lids and these ranged from the plain and functional to masterpieces of the metal-worker's art (figs. 42, 43, 45, 46, 50, 52, 58 and 62). While the lids were mostly unconnected with the subjects of the pipes there are some that complemented them; for instance, a lid shaped like a Chinese hat might be made for a bowl decorated in chinoiserie, or a pickel-haube, the spiked helmet of the old German army, for a military bowl. In some cases the lid was also made of porcelain and was an extension of the object depicted on the bowl. In this group we find representations of animals, birds and humans in which the container represents the body, and the lid, hinged at the neck, forms the head (figs. 59 and 60).

The decoration of the bowls ranged from works of art to the lowest depth of garishness. Even when garish, however, they illustrate the tastes of a certain social class in their period

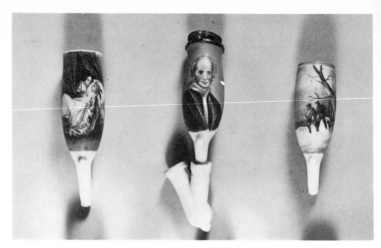

51. (*left*) A fairy tale illustration: 'The Sleeping Beauty'.   52 (*centre*) Leo XIII,
Pope from 1878 to 1903 in German porcelain. Length including reservoir 6 in.
53. (*right*) Out in the snow with gun and dog, transfer-printed on porcelain.
Last quarter of the 19th century.

and deserve a place in a representative collection.

These pipes can be divided into a number of well-defined groups according to the subject depicted, although a few designs may fit into more than one group.

Portraits. These are of men and women, famous and infamous, real or imaginary, contemporary or historical. Here we have rulers, military leaders, beautiful women, writers, philosophers and so on (figs. 42, 43 and 52). In Hood's *Comic Annual* for 1836 appears the story of the Doppeldick household entitled 'The Domestic Dilemma'. It is said of Herr Doppeldick that, 'when he once had in his mouth his favourite pipe with a portrait of Kant on the bowl of it, he sucked through its tube a sort of transcendental philosophy which elevated him above all the ills of human life'.

Copies of Paintings. The picture on the bowl was often but not always surrounded by a gilt line probably intended to represent the frame (fig. 44). For a contemporary account of this group we again go to Thomas Hood who in his *Up the Rhine* published in 1840, describes the crowds going to a Berlin art exhibition and says:

> 'instead of a *Catalogue raisonné* you may go to any pipe-shop to know which are the best or at any rate the most popular pictures by the miniature copies on the bowls'.

Military and Patriotic. Here we have military personalities, suitably captioned battle scenes and regimental bowls with matching sumps and tubes sold in garrison towns and bought as souvenirs of their service days by soldiers or presented by one or more of their comrades (figs. 47 and 48). On these we may find inscribed name, rank, regiment, date and, if presented, the names of the donors.

54. (*above*) Personalized porcelain pipe bowl dated 1860. Decorated in fine gilding.

55. Combined porcelain bowl and reservoir typical of second quarter of the 19th century. Length 4½ in.

56. Convivial scene 'The zither player'. Austrian, late 19th or early 20th century.

Student. These pipes portrayed scenes and objects connected with the extra-mural activities of students belonging to one of the famous societies that engaged in such activities as duelling and ceremonial beer-drinking (figs. 46 and 50).

The Chase. This is rather a large group depicting sporting animals and men out with dog and gun. The most popular animals seen on them are the various species of deer that inhabit the German forests but almost any other creature of sport, including trout, may be found (fig. 53).

Religious. In this category are represented biblical characters as well as people in national costume praying at some road-side shrine.

Fairy Tale and Legend. A preference is shown here for subjects from stories by the brothers Grimm and heroes of German sagas such as Dietrich von Bern and Siegfried (fig. 51).

Domestic and Convivial. This group ranges from quiet family reunions to tavern scenes and village dances, and from pictures of courting couples to valentine-type designs (fig. 56).

Humorous. Satirical sketches, caricatures or slightly *risqué* designs, often with a suitable caption, are included here.

Trades and Professions. Subjects representative of various occupations and industrial achievements come under this heading.

Souvenirs. Views of towns and resorts usually captioned with the name (fig. 45).

Purely Ornamental. This class would include many of the early bowls with decorative motifs taken from nature, and representations

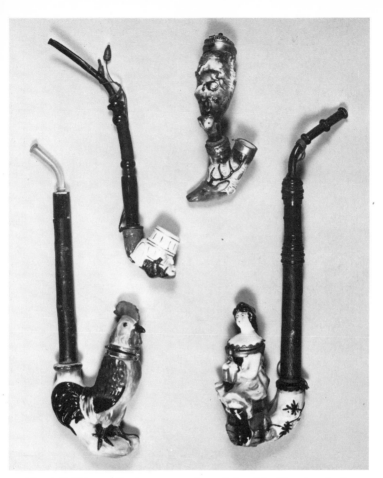

57. (*above left*) Thirsty sailor, horn stem and mouthpiece joined by a length of flexible tubing. German, mid-19th century. 58. (*above right*) Matching bowl and reservoir. Note owl's head on protruding boss near the bottom of the bowl. 59. (*below left*) Fine porcelain representation of a cockerel. The hinged head forms the lid. Wooden tube with horn mouthpiece. German, last quarter of the 19th century. 60. (*below right*) German barmaid in porcelain. Her head forms the hinged lid. Cherry-wood stem joined by a piece of flexible tubing to the horn mouthpiece. Third quarter of the 19th century.

Two early 19th century
German porcelain bowls.
61. (*left*) Depicts people
engaged in countryside
activities. 4½ in.
62. (*right*) Oriental men
and women.

of oriental scenes made during one or other of
the periods when the chinoiserie craze was
sweeping Western Europe (fig. 62).

The division into groups is not intended as a
rigid rule but more as an indication of the
many possibilities open to the collector and
the immense variety of pipes obtainable.

The porcelain pipe never achieved any
popularity in England. A small number were
imported from time to time for sale in a few of
the smarter tobacconists' shops, but it was a
negligible trade. To the best of my knowledge
only the firm of W. H. Goss has produced
porcelain pipes in Britain. They formed part of
their range of armorial souvenirs of various
resorts with the town's arms painted in enamel
colours on the bowl. The reservoir was left
plain but showed the firm's mark on the front.
The cherry-wood tubes were under 12 in. long
and, judging by their style, probably imported
from Germany or Austria.

5.   Meerschaum Pipes

MEERSCHAUM – a German word meaning 'sea foam' – is a translation of *kef-i-darya*, the Persian name for this substance. The German term was also adopted in English while others translated it into their own language – *écume de mer* in French, *schiuma di mare* in Italian, and so on.

The earliest mention of the term in English, as indicated by the *Oxford English Dictionary*, refers to a book entitled *Elementary Mineralogy* by Kirwan, published in 1784 where we find 'Meerschaum of the Germans, Keffekill'. *Keffe kill* (foam of clay) was the name given to it by the inhabitants of Asia Minor, where it was first found, because when newly mined it tends to form a lather with water.

Meerschaum is a light, whitish mineral, chemically a hydreous silicate of magnesium, which occurs in the form of nodules amongst layers of other rocks. The principal deposits are in Asiatic Turkey but it is also found in Tanzania, Greece, Bohemia and other areas. The material, being fairly soft and easy to carve and taking on the most delightful hues when smoked, became a favourite for pipe bowls, cigar and, later, cigarette holders.

It is quite possible that the Turks first used meerschaum as well as clay bowls for their long-stemmed pipes, but the exact date of its introduction into Western Europe remains shrouded in the mists of oft-repeated legends, uncorroborated by contemporary evidence. A rough date might be around the second quarter of the 18th century and the first country to start their manufacture could have been Austria, France or Germany. The industry was certainly thriving in those countries before the end of the century.

An essential feature in the making of these bowls was a waxing treatment which not only prevented the too rapid carbonization of the

63. Meerschaum pipe. The bowl has a silver lid with the Vienna hallmark for 182– (the last figure not clear). The tube is a combination of wood, horn, antler, and flexible tubing. Overall length 21 in.

64. (*left*) Meerschaum bowl with ornate silver lid. Hallmark not clear. Tube is made of horn and tortoiseshell. Austrian, early 19th century.

65. (*above right*) Finely carved meerschaum head of a lady wearing a mid-19th century hair style. Amber mouthpiece. Probably French.

66. (*below right*) Pseudo-meerschaum pipe with brass lid. Tube decorated with mother-of-pearl. The bowl is dated 1810, but this is not an authentic date. Made in Austria in the late 19th century and moulded from meerschaum parings.

meerschaum but also helped the colouring process which formed so vital a part of the ritual associated with its smoking. Great care and skill were devoted to smoking-in or colouring these pipes and many smokers developed their own techniques for obtaining the desired results. One method, according to Fairholt (1859), was to swathe the pipe in folds of flannel so that the line of demarcation between the tints of yellow and brown was clearly defined.

This colouring fetish was already strongly established in Germany by the end of the 18th century. The poet Samuel Taylor Coleridge in a letter written from Ratzeburg near Lübeck on January 14, 1799 refers to:

'A pipe of a particular kind that has been smoked for a year or so, will sell here for twenty guineas. They are called meerschaum.'

On July 10–12, 1843 the sale took place at Messrs Christie's and Manson's of 'The unrivalled collection of Pipes, etc.' belonging to the late Duke of Sussex, Queen Victoria's uncle. Out of over 200 pipes sold 84 were meerschaum and where applicable the caption 'beautifully smoked' appeared in the catalogue. Here are some of them: 'A Meerschaum Bowl with two Lions, beautifully

67. Model of a Negro girl's head. Sold by S. Weingott & Son, 83 Fleet Street, London, and carved at their Gumperdorfer Strasse works in Vienna between 1886 and 1891.

68. Possibly carved in Italy and sold by Righini of Venice during the third quarter of the 19th century as a tourist souvenir of the lions of St Marks.

smoked', 'An Old Meerschaum Bowl, beautifully smoked, silver mounted', 'A Fine Meerschaum Bowl with a map of England', 'Fine ditto of rich colour'.

In *The Diary of a Nobody* by George and Weedon Grossmith, published about 1880, there is an interesting reference to colouring:

'Cummings unexpectedly dropped in to show me a Meerschaum pipe he had won in a raffle in the City, and told me to handle it carefully or it would spoil the colouring if the hand was moist.'

The mystique was still very much with us at the turn of the century; the late Sir Compton Mackenzie, reminiscing on his student days at Oxford in 1901 (*Sublime Tobacco*, 1957), states that:

'many of my contemporaries felt bound to colour a meerschaum. This was a solemn undertaking. Owners of meerschaums in the process of being coloured used to lay them down upon the table more gently than the most anxious young mother would deposit her first-born in its cradle.'

It should not be too difficult even in this age of speed and bustle to imagine the Victorian papa, complete with smoking jacket and tasselled smoking-cap, ensconced in a high-backed armchair, indulging in the contemplative pastime of colouring his pipe.

Meerschaum carving was an art and like all arts had exponents ranging from the genius to the unskilled whittler. This was best expressed by a very old retired carver who was interviewed for an article entitled 'With Vienna's last meerschaum sculptors' published in the *Völkischer Beobachter* of July 30, 1938. The old man, who first put up his sign as a carver in the 1880s, told the reporter that there were pipe carvers and pipe makers and that the

69. Meerschaum claw pipe with amber mouthpiece in original case. It was presented in about 1893 to George Barnes Bigwood (1829–1913), Victorian actor and stage manager at the Britannia Theatre, Hoxton.

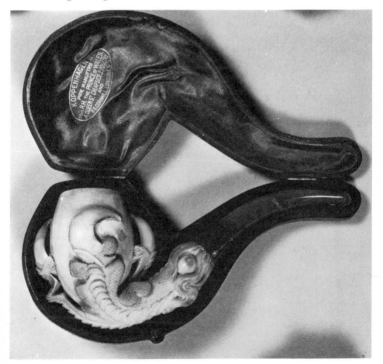

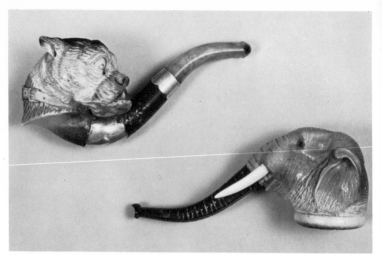

70. (*left*) Meerschaum bowl in the form of a bulldog's head. Amber mouthpiece. French *c.* 1870.
71. (*right*) Meerschaum bowl in the form of an elephant's head with ivory tusks. The vulcanite mouthpiece represents the trunk. Country of origin not determined. Sold in London *c.* 1891–1894.

difference in quality between their work approximated pretty well to that between Michelangelo's and a house painter's.

As with pipes made from other materials meerschaum bowls were often carved to represent mythological characters, contemporary or historical personalities, heads of unknown men and women, scenes of the chase, portrayals of animals, plants, military and other subjects (figs. 65, 67, 68, 70–72). Two designs appear to have been universally popular for a very long period. One of these represents an eagle's claw holding the bowl and the other a hand holding the bowl (figs. 69 and 74). They were made in large numbers from about the 1860s onwards and are consequently fairly common. Being individually made, however, they vary in quality of execution according to the skill of the carver.

In Messrs Salmon and Gluckstein's catalogue for 1899 are advertised the claw pipe with 'block amber mouthpiece in velvet-lined leather case at 21/–' (£1.05) and a 'real meerschaum hand, with best amberoid mouthpiece, in plush-lined case 12/6' (62½p). They also advertise several other models including at 25/– (£1.25):

'The "Arab". The Meerschaum is of the finest quality. The carving of the highest class, and the mouthpiece is faultless. The case is covered with the best Russia leather, and lined with the finest silk plush.'

The meerschaum imported from Turkey was fashioned into pipes at various European centres but principally in Germany and Austria. Among the prize-winners at the Crystal Palace exhibition of 1851, in the section devoted to 'Miscellaneous manufactures and small wares', was the firm of Lux Brothers from Prussia, who won an honourable mention for meerschaum pipes, as did the firm of Louis Bolzau, members of the German Zollverein, in the section headed 'Working in

72. Meerschaum bowl representing a French Zouave soldier wearing the *impérial* type beard made popular by Napoleon III. French 1860s.

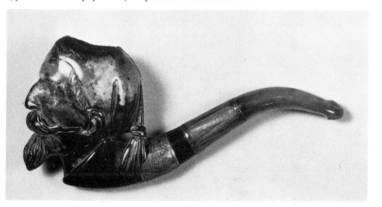

precious metals, articles of virtu, etc.' The *Illustrated Exhibitor*, a magazine published during 1851, praises a collection of meerschaum pipes from Ruhla in an article on the German Zollverein.

It is surprising that there should not be any mention of Viennese exhibitors since Vienna had by that time become one of the most important European centres of the industry both as regards quality and quantity. As early as 1821 Dr Thomas Frognal Dibden, in his *Bibliographical, Antiquarian and Picturesque Tour of France and Germany*, wrote about Vienna's interest in smoking: 'a good Austrian thinks he can never pay too much for a good pipe' and goes on to describe a meerschaum pipe 'made in the fashion of a blackamoor's head'.

The earliest pipes, until about the mid-19th century, generally had large bowls with comparatively short shanks and were smoked by means of long tubes similar to those described in the previous chapter (fig. 64). From the 1840s onwards the bowls gradually started to diminish in size, the shank becoming longer in

73. Meerschaum bowl, amber mouthpiece. Gauntleted hand holding a pickelhaube (the spiked helmet of the Imperial German army) with a Prussian eagle helmet plate. German *c.*1860s.

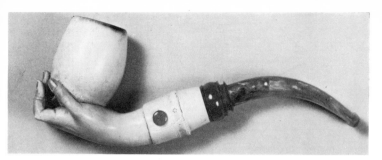

74. Meerschaum hand holding bowl. Amber mouthpiece. Country of manufacture not established. Last quarter of the 19th century. Length 7 in.

relation to the depth of bowl and being fitted with a mouthpiece usually made of amber or an amber-coloured substitute (figs. 65, 69–71, 73–75).

An author using the pseudonym A Veteran Smoker, writer of a little book entitled *The Smoker's Guide, Philosopher and Friend*, published in 1876, bemoans the passing of the long tube of his younger days but admits – if rather grudgingly – that the short pipe has advantages 'when one is playing billiards, or for carrying about in pockets, since people have taken to smoking pipes out of doors'.

Dating meerschaums is not an exact science but a few general rules may occasionally help. If the pipe has hall-marked silver fittings it can be dated exactly to the year, provided the silver is Austrian or English, and approximately when marked in some other countries. However a silver fitting, particularly at the junction of the shank and mouthpiece, could be the result of a repair some years after the pipe was made; in this case the pipe itself would obviously be earlier than the mark.

Where contemporary personalities are portrayed the pipes might be dated after some research through illustrated encyclopedias (the French *Petit Larousse* is particularly useful). If the pipe is in its original leather-

75. Modern meerschaum carved in Turkey in traditional style. Mouthpiece is made of an amber-coloured composition. Bought in Rhodes, 1976.

covered case, with the retailer's name and address inside, a date within the span of the shop's operations at the given address could be obtained by a search through the trade directories of the period. Fashions in dress and hair-styles can be dated by examining reference books on the subject, available in many public libraries.

The industry started to decline rapidly with the outbreak of the First World War in 1914 but it never quite died out. In recent years there has been a slight revival with pipes imported from Turkey, some carved, appearing in tobacconists' shops (fig. 75).

6.   European Wooden Pipes

WOOD, which is readily available in most countries, might appear to be the most obvious natural material for the manufacture of tobacco-pipes. In spite of this it was the clay pipe which dominated smoking for about two and a half centuries following the introduction of tobacco into Europe. Wooden pipes were also being made during this period but in comparatively small numbers.

The earliest contemporary account in England comes to us in one of the manuscripts left by the antiquary, John Aubrey (1626–1697). Aubrey was told by his grandfather that: 'In our part of North Wilts, e.g. Malmesbury Hundred . . . they had first silver pipes. The ordinary sort made use of a walnut shell and a strawe.'

A very much later record in English is found in a letter written on March 18, 1765 by Tobias Smollet, giving an account of a journey from Nice to Turin. He describes an encounter on the mountain Brovis with a strangely garbed Italian marquis who 'had a silk handkerchief about his neck and his mouth was furnished with a short wooden pipe, from which he discharged wreathing clouds of tobacco-smoke'. The appearance of the pipe is, unfortunately, not mentioned.

A good account of German wooden pipes is given in an article published in the February 9, 1856 issue of *Chambers Edinburgh Journal*. The author writes:

'The Germans have perhaps experimented more profoundly in pipes than any other European people. They long used a beautiful pipe carved by the herdsmen and peasants of the Black Forest from the close-grained and gnarled root of the dwarf-oak. The wood is hard enough to resist the action of the fire, becoming but slightly charred by

76. *Ulmer Maserpfeife* – typical burr-wood pipe from Ulm in Germany with cherry-wood tube. First half of the 19th century, overall length 19 in.

years of use. The carvings represented sylvan scenes, boar-hunts, rencounters with wolves, sleigh-driving, fowling and the exploits of robbers. Not unfrequently the subject was an illustration of ancient German literature, as a scene from the story of Reynard the Fox.'

The author of the above gives the impression that these, often very artistic, carvings were produced exclusively by amateur spare-time whittlers. He was obviously not aware of the thriving industry carried out at Ulm on the Danube for at least a century at the time he wrote his article. These bowls, which obtained wide acclaim in their day, formed the subject of a monograph by Adolf Häberle published by Otto Wirth of Amberg in 1950 and entitled *Die berühmten Ulmer Maserpfeifenköpfe* ('The Famous Burr-wood Pipe-bowls from Ulm').

Roots and burrs from various trees and shrubs were used including ash, box, elm,

77. (*above*) Silver inlay decoration on a continental wooden pipe of the third quarter of the 19th century. The hallmark on the silver lid is not clear enough to determine the country of manufacture. Overall length 8½ in.

78. (*right*) Deeply carved hardwood pipe bowl from the first half of the 19th century, representing a forest scene. A dead stag is lying at the hunter's feet. The lid is marked 'Fabery in Wien'.

poplar and sycamore. Some bowls were finely carved while in others the simple beauty of the unusually grained wood was the only ornament needed. The bowls were almost invariably fitted with metal covers and the tubes were similar to those of the contemporary porcelain and meerschaum pipes described earlier (fig. 76).

William Hone in his *Table Book* published in 1827 provides some information on a distinctive type of Irish pipe:

'The bowl part formed of iron, like the socket of a candlestick, is inserted in a piece of mahogany carved in the shape of a violin or a pair of bellows, or some other whimsical form; and the mahogany is securely bound and ornamented with brass wire: to a small brass chain is attached a tin cover for the bowl.'

Also from Ireland came the tourist souvenir bog-wood pipes with bowls in the shapes of cauldrons, acorns and so on, often

79. Hardwood bowl reminiscent of a ship's figurehead. Late 18th or early 19th century, central European.

80. Large rustic cherry-wood pipe with horn mouthpiece. French, last quarter of the 19th century. Length 7½ in.

81. Late 18th century hardwood pipe-bowl. The removable wooden lid is in the form of a hat. The bowl is lined with iron and the short extension of the shank, to which the stem was fitted, is also of iron. Probably made in Switzerland.

ornamented with shamrocks, Irish harps or woolfhounds, with or without the name of a resort in fancy lettering (fig. 88).

Novelty pipes made from a variety of woods in several European countries started to become popular during the second half of the 19th century and are still being produced, but on a very much reduced scale. Some were good examples of regional folk art while in others the bowls consisted of crudely carved grotesque human heads, often garishly coloured (figs. 79, 81, 82 and 90).

It is perhaps apt to conclude this chapter with an account of the most recently used wood in pipe manufacture. It is a wood which has dominated the pipe world on a scale only equalled in the past by clay. This is, of course, the briar.

Some time in the mid-19th century it was discovered that the hard root of a shrubby Mediterranean plant known as tree heath (*Erica arborea*) was eminently suitable for turning into pipe bowls and a new era in the

82. (*above*) Young woman's head carved in hardwood. Note the long shank. The amber mouthpiece is missing. French, second quarter of the 19th century.

83. (*below*) Briar bowl, representing Voltaire, with horn mouthpiece. French, third quarter of the 19th century.

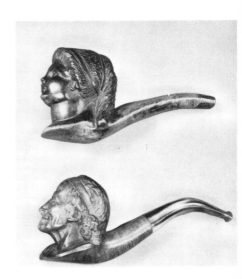

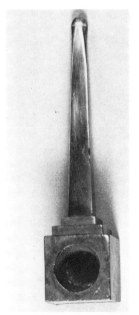

84. (*above*) Briar bowl, vulcanite mouthpiece. Made by the firm of H. Legrand of Rouen, early this century.

85. (*below*) Briar bowl, horn mouthpiece. It represents the future Edward VII as Prince of Wales. Made in France *c.*1890s.

86. (*bottom*) Briar bowl impressed with Cleopatra's Needle and the diamond-shaped registration of design mark for November 21, 1877. It was made in time for the arrival of the famous monument to London in 1878.

history of pipe smoking had begun. This plant is a native of several Mediterranean countries and is called *bruyère* in French; the English name briar was adapted from the French, although the tree heath is in no way related botanically to the wild rose which we also call briar. This new industry started at St Claude in the Jura district of France, a town with a long history of woodcarving.

A St Claude firm, C. J. Verguet Frères, advertising in the *Post Office London Directory* for 1895, stated that they had been manufacturing 'briar-root pipes' since 1857. Other firms may well have been established a few years earlier judging by the thriving export trade that appears to have been established by 1859. In that year Fairholt was able to remark that 'pipes made of briar-root are now common in our shops, but expensive, the bowls costing about three shillings (15p) each'.

The first reference to a London manufacturer of briar pipes is found in the *Post Office*

87. (*above*) Bull's head pipe made in France. This design, made in several countries, was popular from late in the 19th century until well into this one.

88. (*centre*) Bogwood souvenir from Ireland, the bowl shaped like a three-legged cauldron.

89. (*below*) Briar bowl fitted on vulcanite stem. It is inscribed 'The Rugby Pipe, Made in Germany' and has a British registration of design number for 1894. Length 6 in.

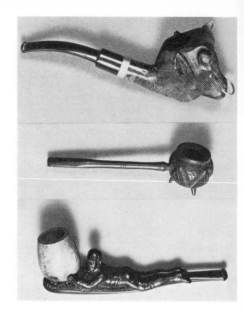

London Directory for 1862. The firm was that of Joseph Koppenhagen, 413 Oxford Street. By 1864 four London makers were listed in the directory and they continued to multiply as the century advanced. The making of a good briar pipe requires numerous skilled operations and by the early years of the 20th century English manufacturers had acquired an international reputation undiminished to this day (figs. 83–86 and 89).

7.   Other European Pipes

Holland. The clay pipe industry in Holland was started by Englishmen and the first of many was William Baernelts, known in Holland as Willem Barentsz, who established himself at Gouda in 1617. He took as his mark a crowned rose and before his death in 1625 other English craftsmen had started manufacturing at Gouda and Rotterdam. By 1637 the Dutch pipemakers in Gouda began to outnumber the English and tried to form a guild to exclude them. Following protests by the

90. Two carved wood souvenir-type pipes from the mountain regions of Central Europe. Their production started in the mid-19th century and continued well into this century. These two items could well be from Switzerland.

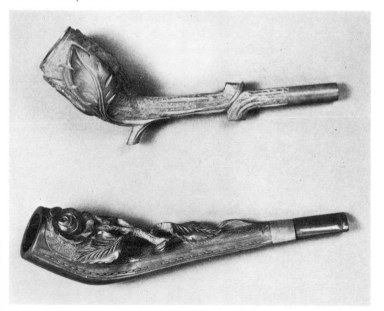

wives of English makers, the authorities refused permission for its creation and decreed instead that every maker should have his own mark. A guild incorporating all makers was eventually formed in 1660.

The decoration of pipes in relief was authorized in 1698 and by the middle of the 18th century about half the town's population was, in one way or another, employed in pipe manufacture. Of all the manufacturing centres in Holland, Gouda became the most important: so much so that the Dutch word for an inhabitant of that town, *gouwenaar*, became a generic name for clay pipes.

The Dutch clays generally follow the form of contemporary English pipes but differ in certain particulars. The great majority of Dutch pipes were marked and ornamentation started much earlier than it did in England; at

91. Two German novelties in brown clay, made for the English-speaking market during the Edwardian era and continued for a while into the 1920s.
(*centre*) 'The Whole Dam Family' and 'Made Abroad' (impressed). The original box is also illustrated (*above*).
(*below*) 'It's A Shame To Take The Money' (impressed).

92. Mid-19th century Danish pipe. The straw-covered plaster-like bowl alone has a length of 5¼ in. The bowl and wooden tube fit into the horn reservoir.

the same time the stems were much more decorated than those of English pipes.

Italy. In Italy wood and meerschaum were as popular as in other Western countries but in clay they appear to have had a predilection for pipe bowls made of a red variety found in various parts of the country and smoked by means of tubes made from some sort of reed. Uniquely, Italian bowls were made from lava in the Neapolitan region. Lava is the molten material ejected by volcanoes which, in cooling, takes many forms. The particular stone used for these pipes was a compacted form of volcanic ash ranging in colour from a greeny-grey to brown. A variety of trinkets as well as pipe bowls was carved from it between about the 1840s and the 1870s. The favourite designs were classical heads and characters from medieval Italian comedy and drama. The bowls were often provided with metal lids and the stems varied according to taste (fig. 96).

Denmark has produced at least one distinc-

93. Art nouveau pottery bowl with cherry-wood tube, possibly French c.1900.

55

tive type of pipe. The large lidded bowl is made of some plaster-like substance and is entirely covered in a fine straw basket weave. A threaded extension at the base of the bowl enables it to be screwed into a horn reservoir with two openings; the other opening is for the tube or stem (fig. 92).

Lapland. From here we get pipes with bowls made from reindeer antler and engraved with designs reminiscent of those found on the Laplanders' national costume – reindeer, sleighs and so on (fig. 96).

Poland. I end this random, but somewhat limited, European journey with an attractive little pipe from Poland. The pottery bowl is totally covered with ornate brass in which much of the decoration consists of numerous small rings. The domed lid is occasionally surmounted by a brass cockerel. The short wooden stem is usually bent into an S-shape and embellished with pokerwork (fig. 98).

94. Two pottery pipes from Schemnitz, now in Czechoslovakia, then part of the Austro-Hungarian Empire. (*above*) made by the firm of Partsch. (*right*) Black pottery made by Selmecz. Second half of the 19th century.

56

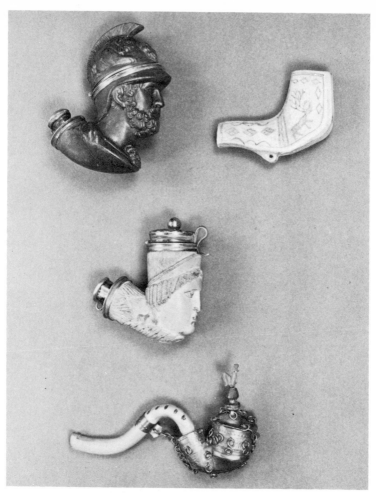

95. (*above left*) Classical head of cast iron with silver fittings. The hinged helmet has a number of perforations which enable the pipe to draw. Italian mid-19th century.   96. (*above right*) Engraved bowl from Lapland made of reindeer antler.   97. (*centre*) Italian mid-19th century classical head carved from lava. Unmarked silver lid and shank fitting.   98. (*below*) A pipe from Poland with a brass-covered wooden bowl.

8.   Hints on Collecting and Price Guidelines

WHETHER you are a new pipe collector or an old hand you should treat yourself, if you have not already done so, to the unique experience of visiting the House of Pipes at Bramber in Sussex. Situated a few miles inland from Shoreham-by-Sea near Brighton, it is a fascinating museum which can be visited throughout the week. The owner and genial host is Tony Irving, a collector for more than thirty years, whose enthusiasm is infectious. Here, in addition to thousands of pipes of every kind, can also be seen an enormous variety of smoking bygones ranging from match receptacles to tobacco-jars, from cigarette cards to large advertising posters, and much more. There are many other collections on public display in England, on the Continent and in the U.S.A. all worthy of a visit, but space limitations restrict me to my favourite.

The decision to collect generally or to concentrate on a particular group such as clays, porcelains or military subjects is entirely a matter of individual choice. The excitement of the hunt and the sources of pipes are, however, the same in both cases. These sources are antique shops, antique markets, fairs, second-hand shops and auctions. There are specialists

99. (*right and facing page*) Three cherry-wood grotesques from Austria *c.*1920–1930.

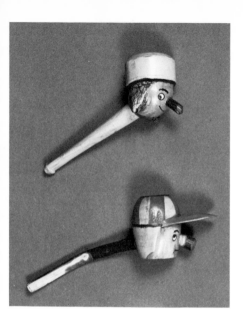

dealing exclusively in old pipes and other associated items but these are usually found only in large towns.

Always look for well carved, moulded, painted or printed specimens. These will be dearer but their aesthetic appeal will more than compensate for the extra cost. Some collectors may prefer to own several somewhat damaged items for every perfect specimen their budget will allow and this too is a valid point of view.

We now come to the vexed question of prices and let me say at once that there is no magic formula for determining the value of a pipe. The saying in the antique business that an object is worth as much as one is prepared to pay for it applies to pipes even more than to most things. Consider the enormous variety in so many materials and the range of skills employed, and the difficulty of accurate pricing

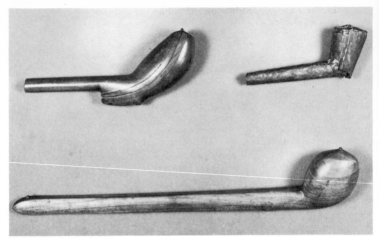

100. Three pipe cases used to protect clay pipes.
(*above left*) Wooden case possibly from Holland, late 18th or early 19th century.
(*above right*) Made from iron and bought with a label attached stating 'Pipecase made by Edward Murrie about the year 1850. Grandfather of Andrew Murrie, Engine Driver. Resided at Park Neuk, Kinross-shire'. (*below*) Fine grained wood, one foot long. Contains a plain clay pipe by Gambier. Late 19th century.

becomes obvious. Any figures given here must be regarded as very elastic.

At the lower end of the scale we have the English clays. The hobby of digging in old refuse dumps has grown enormously in the last decade and thousands upon thousands of broken clay pipes have been excavated in the process. Clay bowls should only be bought if at least an inch or two of stem is still there and then only if they have a mark and/or interesting decoration. Such bowls generally cost under 50p but complete pipes representing contemporary personalities in good condition and marked with the name of the maker, cost between about £8 and £12. The very large pipes up to 9 in. long with bowls up to 3 in. deep, made mostly during the second half of the 19th century would cost, if perfect, between £15 and £25, depending on the subject depicted and its rarity.

When it comes to French clays one should not pay more than say £10 for the very common Jacob bowl, complete with its cherry-wood stem. A rarity, such as Duméril's bowl lampooning the Duke of Wellington's anti-tobacco edicts (fig. 29) would make about £50 or £60 in auction. There is a whole price range between this and the cheaper 'Jacob' but many of the bowls should come below £20.

The average porcelain pipe-bowl might possibly be bought within the £5 to £25 bracket but if it depicts a military subject and is complete with the reservoir and long tube decorated *en suite*, it could well reach £100 or more. The 18th century masterpieces from such factories as Meissen and Nymphenburg are avidly sought by collectors of porcelain, not because they are pipes but because they are examples of a particular artist's work, and here the sky is the limit.

Meerschaum pipes were luxury items in their day and always comparatively dear. Unless you have an unlimited income you can forget the large elaborately carved groups and stick to the many finely designed heads or simple scenes. One of these in good condition with a genuine amber mouthpiece and in its original case might be obtained in the £40 to £100 range while the model of a claw holding the bowl, which is fairly common, might cost about £30.

A final word of advice: always buy a pipe because you like it and can afford it. Do not regard it as a form of investment, which it may well become, but rather think of it in terms of the lifelong pleasure it will give you.

Books for Further Reading

General

Apperson, G. L. *The Social History of Smoking*, Ballantyne Press, London 1914.

Blondel, Spire *Le Livre des Fumeurs et des Priseurs*, Henri Laurens, Paris 1891.

Böse, Georg *Im Blauen Dunst*, Deutsche Verlag-Anstalt, Stuttgart, 1957.

Brongers, G. A., *Pijpen en Tabak*, C. A. J. van Dishoek, Bussum, 1964.

Dunhill, Alfred *The Pipe Book*, Arthur Barker, London, 1924, 1969.

Fairholt, F. W. *Tobacco: Its History and Associations*, Chapman Hall, London, 1859 and 1876. Reprinted Singing Tree Press, Detroit, USA, 1968.

Mackenzie, Compton *Sublime Tobacco*, Chatto and Windus, London, 1957.

Rapaport, Benjamin *A Tobacco Source Book*, Long Branch, N.J., 1972.

—— *A complete guide to collecting Antique Pipes*, Schiffer Publishing, Exton, Penn., 1979.

English Clay Pipes

Atkinson, David and Oswald, Adrian, *London Clay Tobacco Pipes*, Oxford University Press, 1969.

Fresco-Corbu, Roger 'The Rise and Fall of the Clay Pipe', *Country Life*, London, May 21, 1964.

Oswald, Adrian 'Clay Pipes for the Archaeologist', *British Archaeological Reports* 14, Oxford, 1975.

Other English Pipes

Edings, C. A. 'The Thornton Wills Collection of Tobacco Pipes', *The Connoisseur*, London, April 1931.

Macartney, M. H. H. 'Old English Pipes', *The Connoisseur*, London, Sept. 1906.

French Clay Pipes

Jean-Léo *Les Pipes en Terres Françaises*, Le Grenier du Collectionneur, Brussels, 1971.

German Porcelain Pipes

Fresco-Corbu, Roger 'The Art of the German Porcelain Pipe', *Country Life*, London, February 28, 1963.

—— 'German Porcelain Pipes', *Antique Dealer and Collectors Guide*, London, July 1972.

Meerschaum

Raufer, G. M. *Die Meerschaum und Bernsteinwaren Fabrikation*, A. Hartleben, Vienna, 1876.

Wooden Pipes

Häberle, Adolf *Die berühmten Ulmer Maserpfeifenköpfe*, Otto Wirth, Amberg, Oberpfalz, 1950.

Pinto, Edward H. *Wooden Bygones of Smoking and Snuff Taking*, Hutchinson, London, 1961.

Dutch Clays

Goedewagen, D. A. and Helbers, G. C. *'De geschiedenis van de pijpmakerij te Gouda'*, *Monographiae Nicotianae*, Gouda, 1924.

Laansma, S. *Pijpmakers en pijpmerken 1724–1865*, Gysbers en Van Loon, Arnhem, 1977.

Bold numbers refer to illustrations